STUDENT UNIT GUIDE

AS English Language
UNIT 1

Specification B

Module 1: Introduction to the Study of Language

Hazel Norman and Sybil Oakley

Series Editor: Tim Shortis

AS English Language

With thanks to students from Penketh High School, Warrington

Philip Allan Updates
Market Place
Deddington
Oxfordshire
OX15 0SE

Tel: 01869 338652
Fax: 01869 337590
e-mail: sales@philipallan.co.uk
www.philipallan.co.uk

© Philip Allan Updates 2004

ISBN 0 86003 916 1

All rights reserved; no part of this publication may be reproduced, stored in a retrieval system, or transmitted, in any form or by any means, electronic, mechanical, photocopying, recording or otherwise without either the prior written permission of Philip Allan Updates or a licence permitting restricted copying in the United Kingdom issued by the Copyright Licensing Agency Ltd, 90 Tottenham Court Road, London W1P 9HE.

This guide has been written specifically to support students preparing for the AQA Specification B English Language Unit 1 examination. The content has been neither approved nor endorsed by AQA and remains the sole responsibility of the authors. Questions 1 (p. 50) and 2 (p. 54) and texts B, C, D, E and G (pp. 46–49) have been adapted from the AQA January 2002 English Language (Specification B) Unit 1 paper.

Printed by Raithby, Lawrence & Co. Ltd, Leicester

Environmental information
The paper on which this title is printed is sourced from managed, sustainable forests.

Contents

Introduction
About this guide 4
Studying English language 4
The Module 1 specification 5
Assessment Objectives 6
The exam 6
Preparing for the exam 8
Exam procedure 9

Content Guidance
About this section 14

Addressing question 1
Grouping texts 15
Applying the groupings 25
Groupings exercises 26

Addressing question 2
Lexis 34
Grammar 35
Phonology 37
Semantics 38
Pragmatics 39
Discourse 40
Graphology 40

Questions and Answers
About this section 44
Sample data 45
Student answers
    Question 1 50
    Question 2 54
    Groupings exercise response 59

Introduction

About this guide

The aim of this guide is to help you prepare for the **Unit 1: Introduction to the Study of Language** examination. It is intended as a revision aid, not a textbook. There are three sections to this guide:

- **Introduction** — this outlines the Unit 1 specification, and explains the exam format. It gives advice on how to prepare for the exam and the procedure to follow on the exam day.
- **Content Guidance** — this provides a guide to the terminology and ideas you need to be successful in this module, and offers advice on how to apply them. As well as pointing out common errors to avoid, it includes an exercise which will help you prepare for the exam.
- **Questions and Answers** — this includes sample texts and questions typical of those you will encounter in the Unit 1 exam. This is followed by examples of A- and C-grade candidate answers. These are interspersed with commentaries from the examiner which highlight the strengths and weaknesses of each answer. The Question and Answer section ends with a response to Exercise 2 on p. 28 of the Content Guidance section.

Studying English language

A-level English Language is an approach to language study that always starts with texts from everyday life, including varieties of speech, writing, books, magazines, mobile phone conversations, radio scripts and internet chat. The key idea to bear in mind is that language varies because people and situations vary. Your role as a language student is to describe the features and patterns of texts, and to explain these in relation to context.

Unit 1 is an introduction to the study of English Language at A-level. You are required to demonstrate techniques for approaching language objectively and methodically. In the unit test this means showing that you are able to develop some comparisons when you encounter a variety of texts. You will also need to be able to describe significant language features and to explain these in relation to the situations in which the texts are produced and understood.

A-level English Language builds on your work at GCSE but it covers areas of study which you will not have encountered before, including the study of transcripts of speech, dialect and ephemeral texts. It also requires a more systematic approach to describing language.

Below are some comments from students in their first term of the AS English Language course:
- 'It's nothing like GCSE' (year 12 student)
- 'It's all about grammar. I never did that at school' (adult evening class student)
- 'There's so much terminology to learn' (year 12 student)
- 'I'll never have enough time to take all this in!' (mature student)

These comments may reflect your own feelings and thoughts about the course. AS English Language is not an easy option and students often find Unit 1 daunting at first. This is probably because the non-literary texts you studied at GCSE were limited to leaflets, newspapers and magazine articles. You may not have encountered transcripts of spoken English, which can appear complicated the first time you study them. Nor will you have been required to master the complex terminology necessary for analysing texts set at AS, particularly for spoken transcripts. However, the more familiar you become with a variety of texts, the more confident you will feel about applying the terminology. With application and practice you should be able to achieve the grade you deserve.

The English Language course will help you develop an interest in and an ability to examine how language is used in the real world. Even if you decide not to continue your studies to A2, studying English and how it works should equip you with the ability to appreciate and analyse the complexities of language.

The Module 1 specification

Five related concepts form the basis of Module 1. They are:
- **register** — how language varies in relation to audiences, purposes and contexts
- **mode** — how language may vary as a consequence of the channel of communication (speech, writing and mixed modes)
- **idiolect** — the language styles acquired by individuals as a result of life experience
- **dialect** — the variation in language produced as a result of local community and regional diversity
- **sociolect** — language variations produced by the effects of education, class, systems of belief, occupation and membership of any other social groups

This module provides you with the skills, knowledge and understanding which you need for the rest of your course. The terminology you learn for Module 1 will be used in:
- Module 2: Language and Social Contexts
- Module 4: Investigating Language
- Module 6: Language Development

Your ability to communicate clearly to the examiner your knowledge, understanding and insight, using the appropriate terminology, is one of the objectives of Modules 2, 4 and 6. These skills can also be transferred to other subjects you are studying or might wish to study in the future.

AS English Language

Assessment Objectives

Your answers are marked according to Assessment Objectives. These are the criteria examiners use to identify and measure the different knowledge, understanding and skills you have shown. The Assessment Objectives for Module 1 are as follows:

AO1   communicate clearly the knowledge, understanding and insight appropriate to the study of language, using appropriate terminology and accurate and coherent written expression

AO3i use key features of frameworks for the systematic study of spoken and written English

AO4   understand, discuss and explore concepts and issues relating to language in use

AO5i distinguish, describe and interpret variation in the meanings and forms of spoken and written language according to context

Examiners mark your work by considering the relevance of your answer and your engagement with the texts on the exam paper. Other factors include the quality of expression, the quality of the description, the use of ideas from language study and your awareness of the situations in which the texts are produced and received. These ideas can be summarised by the acronym REDUCE:

Relevance
Expression (10)
Description of language patterns (10)
Understanding of ideas from language study (5)
Contextual understanding (10)
Engagement with texts

The numbers in brackets show how many marks out of the total 35 each of these elements is worth.

The exam

Unit 1 is assessed by a written exam lasting 1 hour and 30 minutes, which is worth 35% of the total AS mark, and $17\frac{1}{2}$% of the total A-level mark.

The exam consists of two questions, both of which are compulsory. There are between seven and nine texts on the exam paper for you to use to answer these questions. Two of these will always be spoken English of some kind, and you *must* answer on one of these spoken texts in detail for question 2. Failure to answer on a spoken text will cost you valuable marks. Both questions carry 35 marks, so you must allocate your time carefully. One way of using the exam time might be to spend:

- 20 minutes reading the texts, making notes and planning your answers
- 35 minutes writing the answer to the first question
- 10–12 minutes writing on each text for question 2

Question 1

This question asks you to compare the texts and discuss the ways in which they can be grouped and categorised. You are required to give reasons for your choices too.

Remember to consider the following points:
- Be careful to focus on the question. Don't slip into general stylistic accounts.
- Don't write a lengthy analysis of any text that you intend to write about in your answer to question 2.
- Avoid broad or simple groupings, such as spoken vs written, unless you have something perceptive to say about them. Show that you understand why any labelling of texts is problematic.
- Avoid the 'sequential survey' approach, where candidates write a paragraph about each text in turn — make explicit links between texts rather than implicit ones.
- Make sure you include coverage of most of the texts. You may leave out one or two but no more.

Question 2

This question asks you to select *one of the specified spoken texts* and any *two* others. You are required to analyse the linguistic features of each of these texts individually, and to explain how these are affected by the **contexts** in which they have been spoken or written. You will be asked to apply some of the following frameworks:
- lexis (words)
- grammar (the means by which words are put in meaningful combination)
- phonology (sounds)
- semantics (meaning)
- pragmatics (underlying meaning)
- discourse (principles of arrangement)
- graphology (layout, including drawings, pictures, fonts)

When answering question 2, you should also consider the following:
- Think about how texts work in the 'real world' and understand that context is hugely important to understanding the meaning of a text.
- Be open to new ways of thinking. For example, the answers to the May 2002 exam included excellent work exploring how the intended audience of *Sugar* — teenage girls — would have affected the lexical, grammatical and pragmatic features of the magazine's horoscope.
- Remember that question 2 doesn't ask you to *compare* the three texts you are analysing, so you should write about each in turn.
- Remember that you are not being asked to evaluate the quality of the texts.

To answer the questions effectively you must assimilate a large amount of information in a short space of time. It is therefore vital that you practise, and reflect on this practice, as much as you possibly can. This guide will help you to do this.

AS English Language

Deconstructing the exam questions

The basic format of the two questions remains the same; it is only the texts that vary. An example of the questions is given below, along with some advice on how to approach the two tasks.

> The texts will be fairly short and will cover a wide range of genres. Spoken and written modes will probably be represented equally.

> That is a total of three texts to analyse — only write about one stipulated by the question.

> There is no need to write about all of the features given in the framework — only 'some…where appropriate'. Concentrate on the obviously relevant and/or foreground features.

1 Study the texts A–G. These extracts illustrate different varieties of language use.

Discuss various ways in which these can be grouped, giving reasons for your choices.

2 Taking **either** text C **or** text E and any **two** of the remaining texts, analyse some of the language features of these texts and explain how these are affected by context.

Use **some** of the following frameworks **where appropriate**:
- lexis
- grammar
- phonology
- semantics
- discourse
- pragmatics
- graphology

> Question 1 does not require a close stylistic analysis — that comes in question 2.

> Avoid any overlap of texts used for close analysis in question 2 being the subject of detailed attention in question 1. It may pay to plan your answer to question 2.

> Note the key word 'context' — this is a hint to look at the register used by a writer or speaker. It also suggests a context of reception as well as a context of production.

Preparing for the exam

To be successful in the Unit 1 exam you will not be revising in the ordinary sense. You will not be learning a set of factual notes to reproduce in the exam as evidence of study. The exam tests skills and understanding as well as knowledge, and these are developed during your course through practice.

The best way to prepare yourself for this exam is to develop a thoughtful awareness of all language use around you, both written and spoken.

Written English

Simply looking around your home and school or college can provide you with useful examples of written English. Consider the amount of junk mail we all receive. If you were to collect some examples of this over a week or so, and then looked at them from a linguistic viewpoint, you would be doing some very useful exam preparation.

This exercise could be extended to all kinds of written English around you, such as:
- newspapers (e.g. editorials, news items, headlines)
- magazines (e.g. stories, features, special interests)
- letters (official and personal)
- postcards
- valentines
- birthday and Christmas cards
- children's comics and storybooks
- bus/train tickets
- travel brochures
- e-mails
- recipes
- knitting patterns
- cereal packets

Think of all the ways in which you could work with these different kinds of texts.

Spoken English

Spoken English is more difficult to collect. Unless you carry a tape recorder around with you or have an excellent memory, conversations will remain ephemeral. However, by training yourself to listen carefully to the accent, dialect and idiosyncrasies in people's speech, you will gain experience of 'diagnosing' that speech and not be fazed when you are confronted with transcripts. Try not to eavesdrop too conspicuously, but instead train yourself to register different patterns of speech. Here are a few situations which might provide useful opportunities for reflection:
- family meal times
- chatting on the bus
- interviews (e.g. with a boss, teacher or counsellor)
- telephone conversations (both formal and informal)
- discussions at work or in the classroom

Television and radio can also be useful sources of a wide variety of scripted or spontaneous spoken English. The next time you record a programme, try playing it back and transcribing some of the speech. This is a challenging task, but it will certainly help you to learn how language works.

Exam procedure

Come to the examination with an open mind. By all means have some ideas about possible groupings for question 1, but don't try to work to a prescriptive formula. Don't, for example, assume that the spoken text will always be spontaneous speech. It could be scripted dialogue from a television soap opera, in which case a checklist of the features of unplanned speech would not apply.

AS English Language

Remember that the highest level of achievement in this examination comes from candidates who show that they can think independently and who are confident enough to explore what they find interesting and relevant in the texts.

Before you begin

Read all the information provided
Read the exam paper through to get a feel for the type of texts, their length and any useful features.

Scan the rubric for information such as the date of an extract, the number of people involved and their names. Even the title of a piece can be helpful. For example, an extract from a short story entitled 'The Bloody Chamber' might suggest elements of the horror genre. Look at the origin of the text. If it was published in the USA, this will give clues about the language and the spelling used. A text written for children has different implications from a conversation between two professors.

Examine the texts
Read the texts through carefully, annotating them for any features and patterns that seem significant. It is a good idea to subvocalise, i.e. to read the text in your head so that you can hear what it would sound like if it were spoken.

Remember that all the information is given to you for a purpose. If overlaps are indicated in a transcript, that feature might be worth commenting on and developing in your answer to question 2.

Make a plan
This advice might sound elementary, but many candidates do not make any attempt to organise their ideas before they start writing. Their essays therefore do not demonstrate a well-planned, considered analysis. Create a quick plan using group headings and jotting the appropriate texts underneath.

Use your time wisely and keep track of time in the exam. You could divide the exam into 20 minutes for reading and preparing and 35 minutes for writing each answer. Only you know your own work speed, but you must plan to spend time considering the texts before writing answers, and you must allocate your time so that you meet the requirements of both questions.

Writing your answers

Use the information carefully
Be careful not to fall into the trap many candidates are caught in and simply write out the rubric in full as part of your answer. The examiner has read the paper too and knows exactly what the rubric says. You are just wasting time by writing it out again.

Only write about features that can be found in the texts. For instance, if there is no indication of an accent in transcribed speech then it is not important to your answer. Unnecessary speculation does not gain marks.

Explain your points fully
Be precise about your points instead of making generalisations. Make sure you avoid 'feature spotting', especially when answering question 2. Rather than simply presenting a list of features you have found, make explanatory comments which relate features to effects. Similarly, be careful not to use meaningless assertions, because no marks are given for them. Below are some examples of vague comments which less confident candidates often make:
- 'There is a lot of punctuation in this passage...'
- 'This is an example of alliteration...'
- 'The writer uses commas to make the passage flow...'
- 'This speech does not have much grammar...'
- 'There's no punctuation in this transcript...'

Use accurate terminology
You clearly need to include some terminology when you are analysing texts. However, using technical terms without explaining and developing your points does not demonstrate ability. Many A-grade answers do not contain large numbers of sophisticated linguistic terms, but the terms they do include are appropriate, related to their argument and used with clear understanding.

Avoid stereotypes and assumptions
When writing about texts, don't make stereotypical judgements. Many candidates have made this mistake on past papers. If you are given a piece in a regional dialect, avoid taking the prescriptive view that all non-standard dialects are inferior, or making the value judgement that the speaker is uneducated. Similarly, do not state that 'the writer uses bad/incorrect grammar'; you should refer to it instead as 'non-standard grammar'. Many candidates also make assumptions about gender when it is not relevant to the answer.

The examiner will be looking for your ability to develop a rich interpretation of the text. You need to be able to identify features and patterns and relate these to the factors which cause them and their effects. Interpretations that are subjective, evaluative or judgemental have little place.

Content Guidance

This section covers the terms and concepts with which you need to be familiar for the Unit 1 exam. The information you need to answer question 1 is dealt with first. The different ways in which you can arrange texts are outlined, together with advice on how to apply those groupings. This is followed by a selection of texts, which you can use to practise applying the groupings yourself.

The frameworks you must apply to texts when answering question 2 are also covered. Examples are given to demonstrate the type of observations your answers need to include.

Addressing question 1

Grouping texts

For question 1 you are expected to be able to group texts in a way that shows understanding based on language study. You may already have ideas about groupings from your work for GCSE — formal vs informal, spoken vs written, literary vs non-literary, for instance — but at AS you must show a more sophisticated way of thinking. However, all groupings have advantages and disadvantages. Groupings can help to organise your thinking, but they can also lead to oversimplifying the texts.

The table below summarises some possible classifications, their definitions and the key areas to consider for each. This should be an aid for your thinking, not a plan for your answer.

Classification	Definition	Points to consider
Register	Variations in style due to context	• formal and informal language • lexis and context • purposes • genre • audiences
Mode	Spoken or written language, or mixed mode	• spontaneity and planning • permanent and ephemeral language
Idiolect	An individual's unique language style	• factors affecting idiolect • language choices
Dialect	A language variety associated with a regional or social group	• dialect vocabulary • dialect grammar • accent
Sociolect	A social, occupational or generational group's language	• field-specific language • slang
Standard and non-standard English	Standard English conventions and variations from it	• dialect • sociolect • slang • field-specific language • patois • ICT text conventions, e.g. internet chat

Register

Levels of formality

Gauging the register of a text means establishing whether it is formal or informal, or a mixture (mixed register). However, the level of formality is not necessarily polarised. Imagine a continuum of formality ranging from very formal, such as a written legal contract with its Latinate lexis and syntax, to very informal, such as a telephone conversation between two teenagers, which uses slang and contractions.

The following summons for speeding is an example of a very formal text:

> In accordance with Section 1 Road Traffic Offenders Act 1988 (as amended by section 22) and Schedule 1 Road Traffic Act 1991, I give notice that it is intended to take proceedings against the DRIVER of the vehicle below for the alleged offence of Speeding (Exceeding 30 mph).

Contrast this with the following telephone conversation between two friends:

> Susie: Hi Helen. How you? Seen any good films lately? Nothing on telly is there?
> Helen: Too true. Only thing we have it on for is the footie and you know what I think of that!

These are two extremes and between them would be many variations. In Michael Parkinson's television chat show, for example, the level of formality of the language used is not fixed. It depends very much on the participants, their ages, their education, and their own linguistic choices. Some may change their language to fit the situation, while others may not. Other texts may alternate between formal and informal language (mixed register).

Lexis and context

Lexis is simply the vocabulary used in a text. The choice of lexis (see p. 34 for further details) can be a marker of the level of the formality of a text, but the context is important too. Words that are taken from dialect and used in a person's everyday speech may indicate an informal register, but if these same dialect terms are used as part of a poem written to a strict metre, the register becomes more formal.

Consider the use of the verb 'link' in the following spoken sentence:

> I'll link you Joan so you won't fall again on the ice.

If you were to insert the words 'arms with' after link you would have the more standard form, but this use of 'link' with a personal pronoun direct object ('you') is still a feature of some east-Lancashire speech today. In the following poem, Edwin Waugh, the nineteenth-century Rochdale poet, uses the word 'link' along with other dialect features. You might like to make a list of some of these features for future reference. Start with the omission of vowels, particularly apparent with the definite article 'the', which is often found in regional English.

> Come, Mary, link thi arm i'mine,
> An' lilt away wi' me;
> An' dry that little drop o' brine,
> Fro' th' corner o' thi e'e;
> Th' mornin' dew i' th heather-bell's
> A bonny bit o' weet;
> That tear a different story tells, —
> It pains my heart to see't.
> So, Mary, link thi arm i' mine.
>
> *By permission of the Edwin Waugh Society.*

Most people's idea of a poem would include a formal structure, and Waugh's poem certainly has this quality. However, Waugh's lexis is informal, colloquial and non-standard dialect, so it would be wrong to say that this poem is a wholly formal piece of writing. Think about the contexts in which you might find the following statement:

> They fuck you up, your mum and dad.

Now consider the line as it appeared in Philip Larkin's poem 'This be the Verse':

> They fuck you up, your mum and dad.
> They may not mean to, but they do.
> They fill you with the faults they had
> And add some extra, just for you.

The impact of the line in this case comes from the fact that highly informal language is used in a poem which is usually perceived as being a very formal piece of writing.

When looking at context, you must consider the impact of words or phrases within a piece of writing. Moreover, you must look at the shared knowledge that a text assumes that the reader has. An example of this is the extract below, taken from a letter notifying the addressee of a prosecution for speeding:

> Section 1 — Conditional Offer of a Fixed Penalty
>
> YOU HAVE 28 DAYS FROM THE DATE OF THIS NOTICE TO TAKE UP THIS CONDITIONAL OFFER
>
> No proceedings will be instituted against you during that period but failure to respond to this notice within that period will lead to proceedings. In those circumstances, you will have an opportunity to have a court hearing of the issue.
>
> a) Sections 75 and 77 of the Road Traffic Offenders' Act 1988 (as amended), provided that where there is sufficient evidence to justify the commencement of criminal proceedings for certain offences and no fixed penalty has already been issued, then a conditional offer of a fixed penalty may be made instead of a prosecution. If you can fulfil the conditions of such an offer, you are discharged from liability to conviction of the offence and no proceedings will be instituted against you. If, however, you do not meet these conditions, you will remain liable to conviction of the offence and proceedings will be commenced against you.

This legal document establishes a formal, impersonal relationship between the writer and the recipient, based on an assumed knowledge of the outcome of receiving a letter such as this. Graphology features like capital letters, underlining and indenting make the letter look official before a word is read. The Latinate lexis, e.g. 'commencement of criminal proceedings', conveys a sense of seriousness. The use of the conditional (clauses beginning with 'if') implies choice, but the reality is that the addressee has no choice.

The wider social, moral and historical contexts may also influence a text. Consider the UK's national anthem. It was written in the eighteenth century for a king who would be 'victorious', presumably in battle, and his subjects were calling upon God to 'save' him. The social and religious changes which have taken place since then provide a very different context for this anthem in the twenty-first century. You should also consider how the anthem's meaning might alter if it is sung at an international football match, a Unionist rally in Northern Ireland, or at the last night of the Proms.

Evidently, linguistic analysis is not always straightforward. It is a mistake to assume that all written texts must be formal and all spoken texts informal. It is not always easy to be definite about a text's register, and a cautious approach, showing that thought has been given to possible complexities, will achieve a higher grade than dogmatic statements.

Political speeches are good examples of more formal spoken texts. Peter Mandelson's resignation statement (set by AQA in June 2001) is worth looking at if you have access to that paper. However, perhaps one of the most famous speeches of the twentieth century was Winston Churchill's speech to Parliament, and indirectly to the nation, in June 1940 after the evacuation of the British Expeditionary Force from Dunkirk when Britain was facing the possibility of defeat. Here is an extract:

> ...we shall fight on the beaches, we shall fight on the landing grounds, we shall fight in the fields and in the streets, we shall fight in the hills...

Churchill uses the inclusive 'we' here to gather the country as one. He repeats the pronoun four times. Look at the repetition not just of words but of grammatical patterns. Each clause follows a sequence of subject pronoun + verb + adverbial phrase building up to the 'crescendo' of the next statement:

> ...we shall never surrender.

Churchill knew that this speech was of utmost importance and so he had to use all his skill to write and deliver a powerful speech. He goes on to use dramatic language to describe what might happen if an invasion took place:

> ...then our Empire beyond the seas, armed and guarded by the British Fleet, would carry on with the struggle, until, in God's good time, the New World, with all its power and might, steps forth to the rescue and the liberation of the old.

He chooses nouns like 'struggle', 'power', 'might', 'rescue' and 'liberation' which all have emotive connotations. He refers to America as the New World which may seem an outmoded concept now but suggested freedom and hope then. If you can make comments like this, you will show that you have approached a carefully crafted spoken text in a thoughtful manner.

Purpose

There are many reasons for producing a text. It might be designed to do any of the following:
- entertain
- inform
- advise
- persuade
- instruct

It is very rare that a text will only have one purpose, and you should bear this fact in mind. For example, this guide informs you about the examination requirements, but it also gives you advice on how to tackle the question paper. It could therefore be called a **dual-purpose text**.

Genre
Genre refers to the kind of text you are looking at. Different social practices (such as storytelling or advertising) often have different textual conventions associated with them. When several features are found in one text, that text can be classified as part of a genre. It is important to remember that there can be significant variations within a genre; for example, it would be a mistake to think that all recipe books consist of imperatives, bullet points and lists of ingredients. You could test this by looking at recipes from three different types of cookery book and identifying the similarities and differences. When approaching a text, you could consider the following questions:
- Is it a literary extract taken from a novel, a play or a poem?
- Is it factual writing, such as a biography or an instruction manual?
- Is it a letter? If so, it could be a formal business letter or an informal note to a friend.
- Is it advertising material?
- Is it a text written especially for children?
- How can you tell what genre the text falls into?

Audience
Sometimes a text has a very general audience. For instance, most newspapers have a mass audience, although some are more likely to be read by certain socioeconomic groups. You could certainly think of different adjectives to describe a stereotypical *Guardian* or *Sun* reader. Most of us pick up a popular novel or magazine in a bookshop and select or reject it according to our personal taste, interest or prejudice, but the potential audience for these publications is huge.

However, some texts have a specific audience. A text may be written for one person, such as a personal letter, or for a specific group of people, such as a wedding invitation. Some texts are written for a specific interest audience, for example a piano tutor book. Some texts are for particular age or gender groups, such as an extract from the script of the children's television programme *The Tweenies* or an article from *Woman's Weekly*.

You should note that if you are dealing with a transcript of speech, the only audience is the reader of the transcript. The participants are not the actual audience of the transcript.

Mode
The mode of a text refers to whether it is spoken or written. This sounds very clear-cut, but some texts do not fall into either category exactly. For example, an e-mail or a text message, although technically a written text, will have features of speech such as abbreviations and informal lexis: 'Hi Jo! HOW R U?' This kind of text is a **mixed-mode text**.

Spontaneity and planning

Written English has often been given much thought by the writer. On the whole, written text is not spontaneous or interactive, but there are exceptions, such as 'conversations' in chat rooms and notes to the milkman or on the fridge door:

NO MILK TODAY. THANKS

Dinner in oven!

Speech is often seen as spontaneous. A casual telephone call to a friend or a quick conversation with a work colleague is not usually planned, but a politician addressing the media will have given much thought to what he or she has to say in order to avoid being misrepresented. Newscasters have an autocue; preachers have notes for a sermon. You might have been to A-level lectures in which some lecturers read what they had to say whereas others relied on notes or memory. As with formality, there is a continuum from spontaneity to planning, and texts fall somewhere within it.

However, on the examination paper you might encounter a **transcript** of speech, which is a written text recording words that could have been spoken spontaneously or might have been planned. Examples of these two types of speech might be a friendly telephone conversation transcribed for use in an A-level investigation and a prompt sheet for a telesales person, which follows the same planned formula with each client. An interview for a job would follow a similar pattern because the questions would be prepared in advance, and each candidate would probably be asked the same questions, but there would be spontaneous elements, such as the interviewees' answers. There is an example of this on p. 30.

It is worth pointing out here that play scripts are not transcripts. They are carefully crafted speech and as such can be allocated to more than one group — written and spoken.

Permanent and ephemeral language

Speech is often classified as ephemeral because words are spoken and do not exist in a physical form. However, if words have been written down, or spoken in films or television programmes, they acquire a form of permanence. Simply printing data on an examination paper gives it some longevity.

However, do not assume that all written material lasts forever. A flyer advertising goods for sale or places of entertainment is easily discarded and recycled, as are daily newspapers. Extracts from legal documents and well-known literary texts such as the Bible and Shakespeare's plays have more permanence. Determining a text's permanence needs careful thought.

Idiolect

This term refers to the unique language style individuals develop as a result of personal characteristics, beliefs and social experience.

Factors affecting idiolect

Many factors influence the way a person speaks or writes. They include:
- the region in which a person lives
- level of education
- occupation
- age
- catchphrases from the family
- the media
- idiosyncrasies, such as the filler 'you know'

An individual's idiolect is also affected by the person he or she is addressing. Factors include:
- how well he or she knows the person being addressed
- the status of the person being addressed
- the nature of the relationship he or she wants to build with that person
- the age of the person being addressed, and the age of the speaker
- the gender of the person being addressed
- the situation in which the people find themselves

Language choices

It is important to remember that the linguistic choices we make, consciously or unconsciously, are related to the social situation we are in. Some of the language choices we make are unconscious, for instance in a spontaneous conversation, but many are deliberate or have a specific purpose.

For example, if you need to ask someone for help, you can choose from a number of ways of phrasing your request. You can be very **direct** in an emergency or in a dangerous or awkward situation. If someone collapsed in the street and you needed to find a telephone, you could run to the nearest house, knock on the door and shout:

> HELP! There's been an accident! I need to use your phone!

If you were working with a colleague moving furniture and a table slipped, you might shout:

> HEY! WATCH OUT! Hold that end before it drops on your toe!

You could be **indirect** if you know that the person you are asking for help is very busy and has little spare time. You might use 'hedges' and **politeness strategies**:

> I know you're very busy, but please could you help me tidy this room.

> I'm sorry to bother you but I really need some help.

You may not really want to ask the other person for help, so to 'save face' you could adopt an **ironic tone**:

> OK, so how would you do it?

These are all everyday examples. You need to train yourself to be alert to these linguistic signals wherever you are, and to practise deciding which language choices have been made, why, and with what consequences. These principles apply equally to written texts.

Dialect

At A-level, the term 'dialect' encompasses accent, dialect vocabulary and dialect grammar. These comprise the language variety associated with a particular speech community which is usually linked geographically. Examples include Liverpudlian and Estuary English. Standard English is a dialect too. Below is an example of Gloucestershire dialect:

> I seed the advertisement in the newspaper and our dad said to I, 'If thee carsn't do that as good as some of the men, that's a poor job.'

To achieve a high grade, you should include specific references to dialectal features rather than making generalisations. For the above example, it would be worth noting how the subject pronoun 'I' is used as the object, whereas standard English would use 'me'. The past tense 'seed' is used in place of the standard 'saw'.

Accent

A common mistake is to confuse the terms dialect and accent. Accent refers to the way you pronounce your words. For instance, the short 'a' sound in 'past' and 'last' is an indicator of a northern English speaker. The most common error when discussing accent and dialect is to refer to Received Pronunciation (RP) as if it were standard English. RP is an accent and not a dialect.

Slang and dialect

Some words begin as dialect words but when they start to be used outside the regional area they become slang. For example, the word 'gobsmacked' used to be thought of as a Lancashire dialect term (and was specified as such in an A-level textbook) and is now widely used. Slang is informal language in popular use that is fashionable for a short time, and is often replaced rapidly by newer words. The abbreviation 'fab' and the word 'groovy', for example, were popular in the 1970s because of their association with pop music, but were replaced by such terms as 'wicked' by the 1990s and 'bad' in the early twenty-first century. It is worth noting that the use of opposites such as 'bad' for 'good' is a recent phenomenon.

Slang is often particular to certain age or social groups. For example, during the Second World War, RAF personnel had their own slang terms and cockney rhyming slang is still used in some parts of east London. Consider the different words for the police and how they reflect the age of the user. The term 'bobby' is still used by many older people today, and this may reflect its users' social attitudes. Making a list of all the different words used for the police is a useful exercise in giving you an understanding of slang and encouraging you to think about why those words are used.

Sociolect

This term refers to the lexis and grammar used by a social or generational group. It depends on:
- social class
- education
- beliefs
- occupation
- leisure activities

Field-specific language

Groups who participate in specialised activities often develop a specialised language in order to help them to communicate. This is known as field-specific language. Such language can exclude those outside the group either deliberately or unintentionally. ('Jargon' is another term for field-specific language; it can have negative connotations, so be wary of using it.) Young, male skateboarding enthusiasts, for example, have their own specialised lexis for their hobby. Some of these terms pass into their speech repertoire when talking with each other on a social basis and contribute to their sociolect as a definable group.

A recent study of teenage skateboarders in Manchester illustrates this well. When talking together about their hobby they used expressions such as 'king flip' and 'doing an ollie', which an outsider would not understand unless fully explained in context. One adjective they used was 'gnarly'. This word crossed into their everyday speech to describe anything dangerous, and not just skateboarding activities. It was noted in the study that the word 'gnarly' was exclusive to the skateboarders and was not used by other teenagers. The young men addressed each other as 'dude' and 'man'; both terms originate from the Californian surf culture of the 1970s, which had itself influenced the development of skateboarding.

However, sometimes jargon can seem too clever and elaborate. When he was chairing the 2003 BAFTA Awards, Stephen Fry expressed his horror at having to use the term 'featurette packages' for the clips of the nominated films. 'Clips' itself could be seen as jargon, but 'featurette packages' is not instantly understandable out of context.

Standard and non-standard English

Dialect, sociolect, slang and jargon are all examples of non-standard English. At one time standard English was known as the Queen's English or BBC English. Perhaps the Queen is still a good example of a standard English speaker, as are many presenters reading from a script on a BBC news programme. It is important to get away from the notion that standard English is 'correct' and variations from it are 'wrong' — your role as a language student is to describe and account for variations, not to judge them.

Most educated people can use standard English in their speech and writing but retain some of their dialect and sociolect too. They switch code to suit the context they are in. For instance, English teachers may try to be grammatically precise when writing or even speaking to their students, but at home they are likely to use features of their idiolect.

ICT text types and computer mediated communication

Unit 1 exam papers have included a variety of ICT text types, including e-mail, internet chat and answerphone messages. Other AQA (B) papers have included reference to websites, CD Roms and SMS text messaging, and have also included paper-based texts which feature examples of ICT text conventions such as letter homophones (e.g. 'C U' for 'see you').

In revising for the exam, you need to think through some of the features and patterns associated with ICT text types, and the contextual factors that motivate these conventions. It is important that you develop an appreciation based on the study of actual texts, rather than what is written about these texts in newspapers and other popular accounts. It is often claimed that e-mail encourages 'sloppy', non-standard spelling, and that SMS text messages are full of unintelligible initialisms and emoticons. Some studies have shown that the accuracy of standard English spelling in e-mails depends as much on the audience, purpose and context of the communication as on the text type. One study of text messaging showed that initialisms, e.g. writing 'BBS' instead of 'be back soon', and emoticons, e.g. using ':-)' for a smiley face, are relatively infrequent.

ICT text types are often constrained by the manner of text entry. In most e-mails, web pages and internet chat, text is entered on a keyboard. In SMS a phone pad is used. These constraints may be compounded by the time available in which to write, particularly in communication that occurs in real time (e.g. internet chat). Awkward or time-consuming text entry methods may lead to a pressure to use shortened forms, including the omission of function words and shortened forms of spelling.

Many ICT text types combine features traditionally associated with either speech or writing. In the past, a distinction has been made between communication that is synchronous and that which is asynchronous. Synchronous communication occurs in real time and is associated with speech. Asynchronous communication occurs with a delay between the sending of a message and receiving a reply, as in an exchange of letters. Internet chat is an example of synchronous communication, whereas SMS and e-mail are asynchronous, but often with only short delays between the exchange of messages.

Features of ICT text types

A common feature of ICT texts is non-standard spelling, which reduces the text entry burden of the writer, and which may be used as markers of informality. Typical forms of shortening include vowel deletion and phonetic spellings (e.g. 'nite' for night).

Following from this, some common phrases may be reduced by initialisms or key bindings, in which the first letter of a word in the phrase is used to stand for the word. Another common form of shortening is the use of number and letter homophones ('c' for 'see'; 'u' for 'you'; '2' for 'to', 'two' or 'too'). Many ICT texts include graphological information to help contextualise the linguistic information. 'Smileys', or emoticons, are used to indicate semantic nuances or clues that the words should not be taken literally. ICT text types may have different conventions for marking the presence and identity of participants. In some ICT contexts, such as mobile phones, there may be no mention of the addressee or the writer, because this information is already available on the phone's display. In some examples of internet chat, participants may use elaborate speaker identifiers to suggest a humorous identity. Look, for example, at the names used in the text on p. 47) and consider what is being signalled by them.

Other conventions for ICT texts include pseudo-prosodic features to indicate how the text might sound if it were spoken. Accent features such as 'h' dropping and 'g' dropping are often used in young adults' text messages. The use of capital letters in e-mail and chat can indicate shouting. In text messaging it may not have the same significance. Another speech feature shown graphologically is the keyboard repetition of letter characters to suggest spoken emphasis (e.g. 'so' becomes 'soooooo').

Applying the groupings

Finding similarities

Not all of the groupings can be applied to every set of data on the examination paper. However, if there is only one piece of poetry included, you should not assume that the genre of poetry will not be a group to consider. There might be a text which has poetic language that you could group with the poem. A description of beautiful scenery in a travel brochure could employ techniques used by a poet, such as descriptive adjectives, alliteration, assonance and onomatopoeia. Advertising 'jingles' have a poetic rhythm of their own. For example, in the 1960s the Milk Marketing Board encouraged the public to 'drinka pinta milka day'. This also shows how rhythm can be exploited as a persuasive device.

Cross-boundary texts

A perceptive approach to grouping texts will reveal that there are anomalies. Many texts fit into more than one group; for instance, an entertaining jingle is also meant to persuade the listener to buy more of a certain product. Another example is written texts that have spoken features, such as dialogue in a play or quotations in newspaper reports. An extract or text that can be placed in more than one group can be termed a **cross-boundary text**.

AS English Language

Finding differences

To demonstrate high-level ability, it is important that you look at the texts you have allocated to the same group and indicate where they are different. This shows that you have really thought about the data and have grasped the complexities inherent in this task. Tentativeness is the mark of a better candidate acknowledging that in some cases it is difficult to classify a text rigidly.

For instance, you may indicate a group of texts which all have the same purpose — to inform. They could include:
- an extract from a travel brochure
- the front page of an examination paper
- the back of a packet of instant custard

These texts have other purposes as well as to inform. The first will most likely be persuasive, and the latter two instructive. The graphology they use might be very different. Font size, graphics and layout could vary. The choice of lexis will probably result in different registers. It may be that you can use these observations to link one of the texts to another group which was not so obvious on your first reading.

Groupings exercises

Exercise 1

The table opposite provides a breakdown of the texts set for the first six exam papers for AQA (B) English Language Unit 1. This should give you an idea of the kind of texts you might encounter.

Several conclusions can be drawn from looking at the table. For example, two transcripts have been set on each occasion, and at least ten of the texts have a persuasive purpose. It is impossible to guess what texts will appear on your exam paper, but simply by looking carefully at this table you can practise your exam skills in categorising texts.

There are 12 transcripts in all, but these are not the only texts that could be classed as containing some form of speech. The others include:
- **January 2001:** play; training script
- **May 2001:** politician's speech; some speech in *The Grinch*
- **January 2002:** 'Nasty Nature' speech bubbles; chat room; novel extract
- **May 2002:** sandwich packaging; horoscope; instructions; use of direct address in the poem, i.e. 'you'
- **January 2003:** National Coal Mining Museum advert; cat message; postcard; brother's note
- **May 2003:** Andy Capp cartoon; direct address in Renault advert; direct address in NHS poster

AQA (B) Unit 1

	January 2001	May 2001	January 2002	May 2002	January 2003	May 2003
A	Transcript — three African-Carribbean friends looking at a photo album	Recipe for pesto from an American recipe book	Official letter from Bristol City Council about towing away a car	Transcript of part of a sketch in a television comedy show	Poster for the National Coal Mining Museum, seen at a railway station	Transcript of two colleagues talking together at work on their supposed day off
B	Notice to residents in a hotel bathroom encouraging them to conserve water	Back of a London Underground ticket	Extract from *Nasty Nature*, a book for older children, comprising the opening paragraph and cartoons with speech bubbles	Packaging from a Prêt à Manger sandwich	Notice for bus passengers	Card given by an optician to all contact lens wearers
C	Copyright agreement for an AQA exam paper	Transcript of a monologue of a middle-aged farmer speaking with a Devon dialect	Printout of a conversation in an internet chat room	Two verses of the British national anthem	50-word extract from *The Book of Mini-Sagas*, as part of a *Sunday Telegraph* competition	Andy Capp cartoon, in colour with speech bubbles
D	Opening of 'The Bloody Chamber', a short story by Angela Carter	Letter of apology to hotel residents on Portuguese-speaking Madeira about building work	Advertisement leaflet for a personal organiser, including graphics	Extract for the star sign of Sagittarius from the horoscope pages of *Sugar* magazine	Notice posted through local letterboxes trying to trace the owner of a lost cat	Weather forecast from the Edinburgh edition of the *Metro* newspaper, in colour
E	Extract from *Serious Money*, a play by Caryl Churchill	Transcript of two secondary students and a teacher (Asif, Alan and Mr Chambers)	Opening of the novel *How Late it Was, How Late*, a monologue written in Scottish dialect	Extract from an instruction manual for a mobile phone	Postcard sent from a native English-speaking student, on holiday in Spain, to a friend at home, plus a word processed version	Magazine advertisement for a Renault Clio, in colour
F	Training script for employees selling kitchens over the telephone	Politician's resignation speech, as reported in *The Financial Times*	Transcript of part of a magic act by Wayne Dobson	Transcript of a television advertisement for claiming compensation for an accident; the rubric describes the visuals	Handwritten note left by a 13-year-old boy for his 12-year-old brother, plus a word-processed version	NHS poster in doctor's waiting room, in colour
G	Transcript of a telephone conversation between a student and a teacher	Extract and picture from *The Grinch*, a children's story written in verse, containing speech	Transcript of two friends talking about their children	Back of a till receipt	Transcript of the opening of a mobile telephone conversation between two colleagues	Transcript of an announcement made on a train from King's Cross to Edinburgh Waverley
H	Extract and picture from a book entitled *Care of Leopard Geckos*			Poem 'This Living Hand' by Keats, written in 1819	Transcript of one student interviewing another about his dialect for an English Language A-level investigation	

AS English Language

These are all written texts in which speech features are used for different reasons. In advertisements, speech features can be used to engage the reader — this is usually achieved by using the second person pronoun 'you' or informal language. In personal messages, such as postcards and notes, the register is often informal and can tell you quite a lot about the relationship between the writer and the receiver. Sometimes the language can be exclusive to the people involved, as might be seen in the chat room or in the note from the 13-year-old to his brother. Sometimes the written piece might contain dialect or even a foreign language — the student's postcard is worth looking at here. Perhaps she might be trying to convey how much she is enjoying herself through a mixture of Spanish and informal English.

A useful exercise is to go through the table looking for other groupings; the category of purpose might be a good starting point. Begin with the obvious groupings, but then go on to look for dual-purpose texts and any differences in texts with the same purpose. You should learn a lot about grouping texts even if you don't have the actual data in front of you. If you have access to the AQA exam papers you can go even further with the exercise and look at the detail, especially if you want to look at graphics or register.

Exercise 2

Below is a selection of data collected over a period of 2 weeks by the authors of this guide. Read through the texts and then place them in appropriate groups. An answer discussing these data can be found in the Question and Answer section (pp. 59–60), with which you can compare your conclusions.

Text A

This recipe is taken from the Asda magazine.

FRUITY MOROCCAN LAMB

Serves 4
Ready in 1 hour 45 minutes
Price per serving £1.45
Fat per serving 23g
Calories per serving 500
Fibre per serving 9g

2tbsp Asda pure olive oil
600g lean boneless lamb (cut from the leg or shoulder), cubed
1tbsp Asda ground cumin
1tbsp Asda ground ginger
1tbsp Asda ground cinnamon
1 large onion, peeled and chopped
1 lamb or chicken stock cube
125g Asda ready-to-eat stoned prunes
125g Asda bite-sized ready-to-eat dried apricots
1tbsp Asda clear honey
290g can Asda chick peas, drained and rinsed
1tbsp cornflour
salt and freshly ground black pepper
couscous, to serve

AQA (B) Unit 1

1. Heat the oil in a large pan, add the lamb and spices, then stir and cook over a medium heat for about 3 minutes, stirring all the time. The gentle cooking will bring out the flavour of the spices. Add the onion and cook for another 3 to 4 minutes, until the onion is soft.

2. Dissolve the stock cube in 600ml boiling water, pour into the pan and bring back to the boil. Reduce the heat, then cover and cook gently for $1\frac{1}{4}$ hours. Add a little more stock or water if needed.

3. Stir in the prunes, apricots, honey and chick peas and cook for about another 15 minutes, until the lamb is tender.

4. Blend the cornflour with a tablespoon of cold water to make a smooth paste, stir into the pan and cook until the juices are slightly thickened. Season to taste and then serve with couscous.

Maggie's handy hint
If it's more convenient, you can cook the lamb in the oven at 180C/Gas 4 for $1\frac{1}{2}$ to 2 hours, until tender. Add a green salad for the perfect meal.

Text B

This promotional flyer was hand-delivered to members' homes.

VILLAGE
hotel & leisure club

JURASSIC OFFER!!!

YOUR MEMBERSHIP HAS BECOME EXTINCT!!!

AND WE'VE TAKEN A T-REX SIZED BITE OUT OF THE JOIN FEE JUST FOR YOU!!!

SO DON'T BE A STEGOSAURUS THIS JANUARY!!!

RE-HATCH YOUR MEMBERSHIP FOR JUST £30!!!

(INCLUDING FULL RE-ASSESSMENT)

FOR MORE INFORMATION CALL THE MEMBERSHIP TEAM ON 01925 248408

WE LOOK FORWARD TO WELCOMING YOU BACK TO THE CLUB.

CENTRE PARK, WARRINGTON, CHESHIRE WA1 1QA
TELEPHONE: 01925 240000 FAX: 01925 443240
EMAIL: village.warrington@village-hotels.com
www.VillageHotelsOnline.co.uk

Village Hotels & Leisure Clubs are a division of De Vere Hotels & Leisure Limited. Registered in England and Wales. Registered Office: 2100 Daresbury, Warrington WA4 4BP. Registered No. 418878. VAT. Reg No. 151 651288

Text C

The following text is taken from a commercially produced DVD.

WARNING

The copyright proprietor has licensed the programme (including the soundtrack) comprised in this Digital Versatile Disc for home use only. All other rights reserved. The definition of home use excludes the use of this Digital Versatile Disc at locations such as clubs, coaches, hospitals, hotels, oil rigs, prisons and schools. Any unauthorised copying, editing, exhibition, renting, exchanging, lending, public performance, diffusion and/or broadcast of this Digital Versatile Disc or any other part thereof is strictly prohibited and any such action establishes liability for civil action and may give rise to criminal prosecution.

Text D

This is a transcript from the beginning of an interview between a trainee careers adviser (C) and Graham, a client (G). A brief pause is indicated by (.), a number in brackets indicates the length of a longer pause in seconds, and a vertical line indicates the beginning of simultaneous speech.

C: good afternoon Graham
G: (.)hello
C: thank you for coming this afternoon(.) now er you made the appointment to come and see me so er can I ask what is it you want to talk about today?
G: well (2) I'm taking sort of voluntary redundancy from the job I've got at present|
C: |yeah
G: at the end of August erm sooner than I intended to really (1.0) so my income won't be enough to live on so I want to find something er that will interest me and also bring in some extra income
C: right OK so the main issues are you are taking voluntary redundancy sort of (.) earlier than you perhaps envisaged in the first place and er so you're really wanting to look at possibilities of other employment
G: yeah|
C: |to er to er keep you interested, occupied and give you income
G: yeah
C: yeah OK right (.) we've got about half an hour to have a chat(.) obviously it's your interview whatever you want to discuss we will do (0.5) if you think of anything else apart from what you have just said during the interview feel free to ask me (.) I'll try my best to er answer(.) I'm not promising anything but I'll try my best and er what we say in the interview is confidential (0.5) at the end I'll do an action plan which I'll send to you(.) you can have a look and work through the points that we make|
G: |yup
C: that will be confidential to you and obviously on our computer files as well
G: right OK

Text E

This is a page from a programme for a concert given by the Hallé Orchestra at the Bridgewater Hall in Manchester in January 2003.

HALLÉ
ORCHESTRAL
CHAIR ENDOWMENTS

CHAIR:
A SEPARATE SEAT
FOR ONE

This is a chair in the Orchestra.

During any one season, this chair performs an obvious, yet vital function for a Hallé musician in more than 120 concerts (and many more rehearsals) in up to 20 different venues around the country.

Although on the surface it looks like any other chair in the Orchestra, this one is different — this one doesn't have any support.

By becoming a Hallé Chair Endower, you can help provide a better foundation for Hallé musicians and take your very own seat on the stage!

To find out more please contact: *(name and phone number supplied on original).*

Proceeds from the Hallé Chair Endowment Programme support the Charles Hallé Foundation (registered charity no. 236149)

AS English Language

Text F

Alan, a retired engineer, is going to visit his son Ewan in Canada. He is speaking to his neighbour, Mal, the day before his departure. A brief pause is indicated by (.), a number in brackets indicates the length of a longer pause in seconds.

> Well (.) only a day to go and al be off (.) here's key Mal (.) Joan'll be in to clean at the end of the week (.) told her it didn't matter but she wants to keep the dust down (.) typical woman (.) if you'll put the bin out Tuesday that'll be fine (.) don't bother after this week (.) a'v got your folding stick (.) it's right useful on the plane (.) fits that overhead compartment smashing (.) better than my long one (1.0) hope a'm going to be ok on the flight (1.0) chest's not really right (.) a'v told Ewan if a die he's not to bother sending me home (1.0) he can cremate mi in Toronto (0.5) save money

Text G

This text was accompanied by a photograph of an electric shredder and was on the back of the envelope enclosing the Lakeland Limited mail-order catalogue for spring/summer 2003.

Compact Electric Paper Shredder

No doubt many of you will have heard stories of what can happen if confidential documents fall into the wrong hands. For peace of mind, and to do your best to minimise the risks, it's wise to destroy bank statements, credit card slips, private letters as soon as you no longer need them. Placed conveniently over a bin, this simple to operate, speedy shredder will reduce up to 5 sheets of A4 paper into thin strips, that are absolutely impossible to read. Mains powered. Adjusts to fit different sized waste bins from 12" (30cm) to $15^{3}/_{4}$" (40cm) W.

Ref 5617   £22.95

Text H

This extract is from Caryl Churchill's play *Top Girls* (1982). It is taken from Act 1.

SCENE THREE

JOYCE's *back yard. The house with back door is upstage. Downstage a shelter made of junk, made by children. Two girls,* ANGIE *and* KIT, *are in it, squashed together.* ANGIE *is 16,* KIT *is 12. They cannot be seen from the house.* JOYCE *calls from the house.*

JOYCE. Angie. Angie are you out there?

[*Silence. They keep still and wait. When nothing else happens they relax.*]

ANGIE. Wish she was dead.

KIT. Wanna watch *The Exterminator*?

ANGIE. You're sitting on my leg.

KIT. There's nothing on telly. We can have an ice cream. Angie?

ANGIE. Shall I tell you something?

KIT. Do you wanna watch *The Exterminator*?

ANGIE. It's X, innit.

KIT. I can get into Xs.

ANGIE. Shall I tell you something?

KIT. We'll go to something else. We'll go to Ipswich. What's on the Odeon?

ANGIE. She won't let me, will she?

KIT. Don't tell her.

ANGIE. I've no money.

KIT. I'll pay.

ANGIE. She'll moan though, won't she?

KIT. I'll ask her for you if you like.

ANGIE. I've no money, I don't want you to pay.

KIT. I'll ask her.

ANGIE. She don't like you.

KIT. I still got three pounds birthday money. Did she say she don't like me? I'll go by myself then.

ANGIE. Your mum don't let you. I got to take you.

KIT. She won't know.

ANGIE. You'd be scared who'd sit next to you.

KIT. No I wouldn't.
  She does like me anyway.
  Tell me then.

ANGIE. Tell you what?

KIT. It's you she doesn't like.

Addressing question 2

Question 2 requires you to analyse the linguistic features of one specified spoken text and any two others. To do this you should apply the frameworks outlined below to the texts.

However, not every framework will apply to every text. Graphology might not be of importance in a paragraph from a novel, but if a text included an illustration or different fonts then it would be worth discussing.

You should bear in mind that the ability to comment accurately on grammar and pragmatics will generally gain higher marks than dealing with the more accessible frameworks such as graphology and lexis. Observations such as, 'There is a bold headline to catch the reader's attention' or 'There is a lot of formal language' are not sufficient in themselves. You should certainly identify the more obvious features, but don't dwell on them — develop the point into a more sophisticated analysis.

Consider how different candidates treat the frameworks, whether simple or complex, when you read the sample answers in the Question and Answer section of this guide. Once mastered, these frameworks will be of great use to you throughout your English language course.

Lexis

Lexis is the vocabulary used in the text. When you look at a text, ask yourself whether the lexis is sophisticated or accessible. It is most likely to be a mixture of both. Is it formal or informal? Has jargon or field-specific language been used? Are the words concrete or abstract? Are they polysyllabic Latinate words or shorter Anglo-Saxon words? Are the words related to other words in patterns of meaning (semantic fields)? Sometimes **figurative language** is employed to gain a particular effect. The following extract from *The Big Sleep* by Raymond Chandler (1939) is a good literary example of the use of lexis:

> It was raining again the next morning, a slanting grey rain **like a swung curtain of crystal beads**. I got up feeling sluggish and tired and stood looking out of the windows, with a dark harsh taste of Sternwoods still in my mouth.

The emboldened simile shows not just how the rain looked but its movement. The choice of adjectives (sluggish, tired, dark, harsh) in the second sentence conveys the character's feelings that particular morning.

Having identified the type of lexis being used, try to decide why the writer has chosen it and how the lexical choice can be related to the context of the writing.

Grammar

Grammar is what enables words to be put together in meaningful combinations. It consists of **morphology** (word structure), **syntax** (word order) and **function words** (e.g. prepositions). There are some concepts that are particularly useful: sentence structure; active and passive voice; and word classes.

Do not treat this as an opportunity to write about punctuation, as many candidates make the mistake of doing. As with lexis, you will not gain marks by simply identifying grammatical features. You need to discuss the effect of the grammatical elements and how they can be related to the context of the text. Aspects of grammar you might comment on are discussed below.

Sentence structure

Sentence structure is an important feature of grammar. It may be relevant to look at the different types of sentences used in a text.

Simple sentences

The term 'simple sentence' is very specific. It refers to a sentence which contains one clause and is based on the subject–verb (object) system. Literary texts can use simple sentences effectively. In the following example they are used to create suspense:

> He turned the handle. The door opened. The room was empty. The body had gone.

Be careful only to use the term 'simple' when you are referring to sentences. Do not apply it to every straightforward, uncomplicated feature of language. Some candidates overuse the word and in so doing demonstrate a lack of appropriate vocabulary. Make a list of synonyms for 'simple' and use them in your essays until they become part of your linguistic vocabulary.

Compound sentences

A compound sentence has a series of clauses joined to each other by the conjunctions 'and', 'or' and 'but':

> I got up and had a wash and had my breakfast and went to school.

This is a typical example of a child's early attempts at writing. In analysing this, you might comment on the child's use of conjunctions as a first step to making a narrative. However, for the following compound sentence from *The Big Sleep*, the commentary would be very different:

> I shaved and showered and dressed and got my raincoat and went downstairs and looked out of the front door.

Here the compound sentence, with its repeated use of the conjunction 'and', is used to convey the tedium of Philip Marlowe's everyday routine and is a far more

AS English Language

sophisticated use of language. A higher-level candidate would make this kind of comment rather than merely identifying the quotation as a compound sentence.

Complex sentences

A complex sentence can be used to achieve a variety of different effects. Consider the following sentence from a piece of factual writing:

> In through the concrete passage way with its black iron railings, past the battered grey lift which seldom works, up two flights of concrete stairs which smell of urine and drink, past graffiti plastered walls, and along a concrete walkway, partly blocked by the remains of an old brown armchair, you'll find number 86.

The long complex sentence, which delays the main clause until the end, intensifies the idea of a very long walk past depressing sights and creates a sense of the time this dreary walk takes.

Minor sentences

This kind of sentence is often used in conversation, advertising and notices. It is a sentence which lacks some of the standard grammatical structures, usually a verb. The sentence is understandable within its context. Consider this example:

> 'How are you?' (simple interrogative sentence)
> 'Fine, thanks.' (minor sentence)

Very rarely in informal conversation would you reply with the grammatically correct 'I am fine, thank you.'

Look out for notices which are minor sentences. 'No smoking' is a common example.

Active and passive voice

A signifier of power

The passive is mainly found in legal and other official documents, reports of scientific experiments, various business purposes and in texts which explain regulations, for example on train tickets. It can therefore be an instrument of power. The sentence below, taken from a formal letter about a parking offence, is in the passive:

> The Vehicle was taken into Council possession for a parking contravention.

This is more authoritative than phrasing the sentence in the active voice:

> The Council took possession of the vehicle for a parking contravention.

In the passive version, the emphasis is put on the offending 'Vehicle' (note the capital letter), and the choice of the Latinate word 'contravention' adds to the feeling of power that the Council wishes to generate. A perceptive candidate would be able to demonstrate this kind of understanding.

Creating bias

The passive may be used in biased reporting to hide essential information. This was demonstrated by the coverage of the shootings in Salisbury (now known as Harare) in what was then Rhodesia (now Zimbabwe) in June 1975. The headline in *The Times* read:

> RIOTING BLACKS SHOT DEAD BY POLICE AS ANC LEADERS MEET

The headline foregrounds the victims of the violence, not those responsible for it. Compare the headline in the *Guardian*:

> POLICE SHOOT 11 DEAD IN SALISBURY RIOT

The use of the active voice makes the agents of the action clear.

Word classes

A sentence may contain a large number of adjectives and adverbs, which are relatively easy to identify. Instead of simply listing these features, explain why the writer uses them. If you cannot expand on the use of a particular feature, then you should not include it in your analysis.

Look at the extract below from the first chapter of *Hotel Du Lac* by Anita Brookner (1994) and consider how the adjectives and adverbs she uses contribute to the atmosphere. The narrator is contemplating the hotel bedroom she is to stay in for the next 2 weeks:

> Turning…she contemplated the room, which was the colour of over-cooked veal: veal-coloured carpet and curtains, high, **narrow** bed with veal-coloured counterpane, **small austere** table with a **correct** chair placed **tightly** underneath it, a **narrow, costive** wardrobe, and, at a very great height above her head, a tiny brass chandelier, which, she knew, would eventually twinkle **drearily** with eight **weak** bulbs.

Here the emboldened adjectives and adverbs are from the same semantic field. They suggest a very cramped and uncomfortable space and help to convey effectively the narrator's distaste for the room and her feeling of being imprisoned there.

Comments such as these show more real engagement with a text than simply writing 'there are a lot of adjectives in this sentence'. When you quote from a text, you could underline the exact words you are commenting on in your answer to show the examiner what you are referring to.

Phonology

This term refers to the sounds of words and the pattern of sounds within a text. You are not expected to discuss the phonology of every text on the paper because it might not be relevant. The term is appropriately used to comment on a spoken text or a written text which uses spoken features. You could be told that a speaker had a certain accent, in which case some phonological discussion might be relevant. For instance, the difference between the regional pronunciation of the 'a' sound in words such as 'past' and 'last' might be worth some comment, if it is appropriate.

Phonological features

If you are looking at poetry, nursery rhymes or children's stories and songs, it may be relevant to discuss features such as assonance, alliteration and onomatopoeia. These devices depend on sounds to create a particular effect.

These lines from Wordsworth's *The Prelude* (1798–1800) are a good example of the use of sound:

> All shod with steel, we hissed along the polished ice in games
> Confederate, imitative of the chase and woodland pleasures.

Wordsworth's use of sibilance (repetition of the 's' sound) and the onomatopoeic 'hissed' is very effective in creating the sound of metal skates on ice in this episode from his youthful skating in the Lake District.

Semantics

The term semantics refers to the study of the meaning of a text and how the meaning is made. Here is an example of an everyday conversation.

> Geoff: Hello Jean. Isn't it a lovely day?
> Jean: It certainly is. I think I might go to the beach this afternoon.
> Geoff: What a good idea. Can I come?

This is very straightforward and easy to understand. We are given no indication of anything but the words spoken here, so we can only literally interpret what is said. If we could see the two people, we might get some more clues to the meaning of what they are saying. Paralinguistic features like smiles and handshaking would add to the meaning. These two are friends and glad to see each other. However, if Jean did not want to have Geoff accompany her to the beach, her facial expression might be quite different. If this conversation were part of a short story in a women's magazine, the writer might choose to convey a different meaning. So:

> Jean set off to the shops feeling very apprehensive. She hoped she wouldn't see Geoff Brown this morning. Ever since she had spoken to him at the church garden party he had popped up in the most awkward places. She looked across the road and there he was. Her heart sank.
> 'Hello Jean. Isn't it a lovely day?'
> 'It certainly is,' said Jean although she was really thinking quite the opposite, thinking a bit too hard perhaps as before she realised it she added, 'I think I might go to the beach this afternoon.'
> 'What a good idea,' said Geoff with obvious enthusiasm. 'Can I come?' Jean mentally kicked herself as she tried to think of a reply.

The actual words spoken here are exactly the same but the description of the **context** puts a different angle on the meaning. The simple sentence 'Her heart sank' is a very good indication of Jean's feelings and the meaning of the conversation is influenced by those three words. The metaphor 'mentally kicked herself' is certainly a cliché but it does show Jean's anger at her own stupidity.

If we were to **hear** Jean speak, then her next utterance might convey her real meaning. The emphasis she places on the words could be a good indicator of how she really feels about Geoff.

> 'Well, ACTUALLY I was thinking of taking all the grandchildren with me and as I know you don't REALLY like LITTLE children very much perhaps we can say some other time?'

The words in capitals indicate how the emphasis is conveying Jean's meaning to the reader and to Geoff through her tone of voice.

So the description of the semantics of a text must take into consideration not just the words and the order in which they are presented but the context they are in and, in speech, any other paralinguistic features which might influence their meaning.

One term often used in the study of language is **semantic field**. This refers to words within a particular area of meaning which interrelate with each other. For instance, the various words for items of furniture (*table, chair, bed, wardrobe*) form a semantic field. Words within a particular occupation belong to a specific semantic field, e.g. *diagnosis, prescription, antibiotic* and *surgery* all belong to the semantic field of medicine.

Pragmatics

This term is defined as the underlying meaning of a text — not what it says on the surface, but what is implied. If someone says of a friend's new outfit, 'That's an unusual dress', what does she really mean? Is she being complimentary, or is she trying to hide her true feelings because she thinks it is hideous and does not want to upset her friend?

Similarly, if on a train journey one passenger turns to another who is smoking and says, 'This is a non-smoking area', this really means, 'Put your cigarette out'. The phrasing is neutral and objective in order to avoid confrontation.

A literary example can be found in the extract below from Angela Carter's short story 'The Bloody Chamber'. Carter is on the surface describing the start of a train journey, but her pragmatic meaning is to describe the beginning of a marriage and the awakening of the girl to her physical needs within that context. It employs highly erotic symbols:

> I remember how, that night, I lay in the wagon-lit in a tender, delicious excitement, my burning cheek pressed against the impeccable linen of the pillow and the pounding of my heart mimicking that of the great pistons ceaselessly thrusting the train that bore me through the night, away from Paris, away from girlhood, away from the white, enclosed quietude of my mother's apartment, into the unguessable country of marriage.

Look at the choice of lexis and the use of metaphor. Words such as 'burning', 'pounding', 'pistons' and 'thrusting' convey sexual excitement, and contrast with 'impeccable linen' and 'white, enclosed quietude' which carry connotations of purity and virginity. Think how you could explore the implications of 'the unguessable country of marriage'.

Discourse

'Discourse' is a problematic word because it can be understood in a number of different ways. At AS, it may be helpful to think of it as meaning the study of the principles of arrangement in a text above the unit of the sentence, or in the case of conversation above the unit of the turn. For example, the organisational principles of a diary will be chronological, whereas a government statute will be organised in relation to other types of legal text to which it is related. Some conversations may be organised partly by the nature of the activity which accompanies them, whereas others may be influenced by professional roles and the social expectations of these.

The discourse of a text can seldom be seen in isolation because a text will be related to the circumstances in which it is produced and to other related texts. This gives the secondary definition of discourse in the specification, the ways that 'language is used to express the interests of a particular interest group'. Some texts may combine more than one of these discourses. For example, the Palmtop computer advertisement on page 47 combines the discourse of personal, domestic concerns of family and friendship with a discourse of a sophisticated business worker, along with a discourse of information technology. Identifying the language features which enable this could form the basis of an answer on this text.

Module 1 texts are short excerpts from much longer texts, and discourse features often have to be inferred from limited evidence. To do this you need to reflect on how a text is organised and sequenced, and the relationship of the text to other texts. For the subtle awareness expected from high-level answers, look for the ways in which a text may combine or juxtapose the discourses of other texts. For example, consider some of the genres reflected in mixed-register texts such as the *Horrible Science* books.

Graphology

Font size, layout and illustrations are all features that connect different texts. For some texts, graphology is important, but for others you could be wasting valuable time discussing layout.

Many candidates think that this is an easy framework to use, but this is not necessarily the case. It is not enough to write, for example, 'the author has used humorous illustrations', without explaining their purpose. Look at the example opposite.

Introduction

Science is sickening! Extra science homework is really rotten — but one of the most horribly sickening science subjects is the science of the body. I mean, doesn't the thought of all that blood and all those guts and bones turn your legs into jelly?

Doctors and teachers use a sickening selection of tongue-twisting names for bits you didn't even know you had. By the way — did you know that medical students have to learn 10,000 new words? And you thought English lessons were tough!

But science doesn't just belong to the experts — it belongs to everybody, because everybody's got a body — and you've got every right to know what's going on in yours. Why it gurgles creaks and squelches and other tantalising topics.

And that's what this book is about. The things YOU really want to know about YOUR body. The horrible bits. The horribly interesting bits...

Source: Text © Nick Arnold, Scholastic Ltd 1997.
Illustrations © Tony De Saulles, Scholastic Ltd 1997.

There is much that could be said about this illustration and how it creates humour. There is an attempt to create rapport with the audience of older children through the stereotypical presentation of the teacher, who looks old-fashioned, with her severe haircut and steel-rimmed glasses. The image is anchored to the text, illustrating how teachers use 'tongue-twisting names'. In addition, the heading is written as if by a child, complete with messy ink blots to appeal to the audience further. Comments such as these should help ensure that you reach the higher mark bands.

Questions & Answers

AS English Language

This section provides examples of the type of essays you will write in the Unit 1 examination. The section begins with a selection of sample data typical of the kind you will encounter in the exam, and is followed by candidate responses to exam-style questions based on this data. The responses are of both A-grade and C-grade standard. Each answer is worth 35 marks. It is important that you do not treat these responses as model answers, but rather as a structure and content guide. Before you begin reading the candidate answers, you may find it helpful to make your own notes on the data and consider how you would answer the questions. Then read the candidate answers and compare their ideas with your own.

This section also includes a response to the groupings exercise in the Content Guidance section.

Examiner's comments

Each of the candidate answers is accompanied by an examiner's comment, preceded by the icon ⟨e⟩. These comments indicate what is creditable within the answers and why an A or C grade would be awarded. Pay particular attention to the strengths and weaknesses identified by the examiner, and treat the examiner's comments as useful advice in your preparation for the exam.

Sample data

Text A

This is a letter from a local council's Parking Services department to the owner of a car that has been towed away after being parked illegally.

Vehicle Removal Scheme

Parking Services
Anytown City Council, PO BOX 2, AT01 2AB
Telephone: 01234 567890   Facsimile: 01234 567899

DISPOSAL OF A MOTOR VEHICLE IN COUNCIL POSSESSION

REFERENCE NO. VRS/999/00

To:

MAKE/MODEL
REGISTRATION

23 August 2003

Dear Sir,

Records show you to be the current keeper of the above vehicle, currently at the Anytown Car Pound, Kings Road, Anytown AT01 2AB.

The Vehicle was taken into Council possession for a parking contravention. If you are the owner, or person otherwise responsible for the vehicle, you are required to remove it from Council custody at Anytown Towing 7 Storage Co. Ltd Car Pound on or before 19 SEPTEMBER 2003 on payment of the appropriate charges, otherwise it will be disposed of without further notice.

If you are no longer the owner, or do not wish to reclaim it from the Car Pound, would you please complete and sign the appropriate section on the attached Disclaimer Form and return it no later than 19 SEPTEMBER 2003.

If you do not reply by 19 SEPTEMBER 2003 this vehicle will be disposed of by The Council in accordance with Regulation 14 of the Removal and Disposal of Vehicles Regulations 1986, and Section 101 of the Road Traffic Regulation Act 1984.

Yours faithfully,

PARKING SERVICES TEAM

AS English Language

Text B

This is the opening paragraph of a book about the natural world called *Nasty Nature*, from a popular science series called *Horrible Science*. It was written for older children and published in 1997.

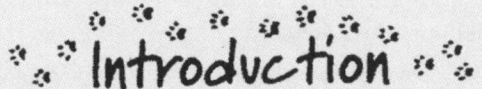

Brute force. Beastly behaviour. Animal cunning. Whenever humans have anything nasty to say to one another they drag animals into it. And animals bring out the worst in some humans, which can lead to nasty situations...

The science of animals can also provide some nasty surprises (and we're not talking about your brutish, wolfish, slavering teacher here). What, for example, about the odd words scientists use to describe our four-legged friends? They certainly leave a nasty taste in your mouth — when you don't understand them.

Source: Text © Nick Arnold, Scholastic Ltd 1997.
Illustrations © Tony De Saulles, Scholastic Ltd 1997.

Text C

The text that follows is a printout of a sequence of messages from an internet chat room. The chat room name of each message writer is indicated by the < > brackets to the left of the text.

<the_rock>yeha that's better hon :))
***Edwin4 has joined #chatterz
<Rizlaskin>HELLO PPL
<dinny> hi riz
***kanibalka has joined #chatterz
<Rizlaskin> HOWS YALL DOIN!?
***PostG has joined #chatterz
<anachroma> nice
***Tittix has quit IRC (Ping timeout☐)
<PostG> hi
***PostG has left #chatterz (PostG☐)
<Rizlaskin> IM FEELING KINDA LOUD 2DAY!
<the rock> ehy caps lock
<the rock> ?? caps
<wip3out> ☐☐2 #☐☐caps = there is a key on ur keyboard called (Caps Lock\). Its on the left side (where 'left' is where ur thumb is on the right side)... would u be so kind to press that key so you don't excess us with your CAPS? Thank you.
***M_SoN_Ve has quit IRC (Leaving☐)
<anachroma> use anticaps :-P
End of #chatterz buffer
Mon Mar 13 17:53:11 2000

Source: IRC chatterz room.

Text D

The text that follows is taken from a leaflet advertising a personal organiser computer.

The Palm™ family of organisers was designed to simplify your life.

No more missed meetings, misplaced numbers or lost notes. In one shirt pocket-sized organiser, you will have everything you need, with you always: your agenda, address book, e-mail messages, to do lists, and memos. With thousands of applications available, the Palm™ organiser you choose can be customised to suit your personal needs and will become the unique companion you'll never want to leave behind.

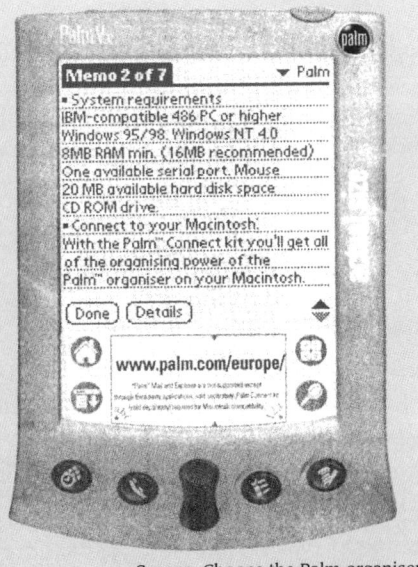

Source: Choose the Palm organiser that's right for you © 2000.

Text E

The passage that follows is the start of the first paragraph of a novel.

> Ye wake in a corner and stay here hoping yer body will disappear, the thoughts smothering ye; these thoughts: but ye want to remember and face up to things, just something keeps ye from doing it, why can ye no do it; the words filling yer head: then the other words; there's something wrong; there's something far far wrong; ye're no a good man, ye're just no a good man. Edging back into awareness, of where ye are: here, slumped in this corner, with these thoughts filling ye.
>
> Source: *How Late it Was, How Late* by James Kelman, published by Secker & Warburg. Used by permission of The Random House Group Ltd.

Text F

Jude is recounting to a friend an experience she had on a recent visit to the cinema when on holiday in Scotland. The length of a pause is marked by the number of seconds in brackets.

> When we came out I discovered I'd got chewing gum all down the side of my trousers. Y'know those black ones I had at Christmas. Must have picked it up off the seat. Bit off really. So I went and complained to the girl in the ticket place. Do you know what she said. She said 'Do ye no have a spare pair with ye so ye can change them and we'll steam clean them for ye?' How stupid can you get. I told her. I said [assumes RP accent] 'I am not in the habit of bringing spare trousers with me to the cinema'. So then, she offered to clean them for me if I brought them in the next day. Well, I told her I was leaving the country tomorrow so how could I do that? Anyway when I got home I wrote to the company and they sent me a letter offering to clean them if I posted them. Would pay postage and so forth. Seems a bit of a hassle to me but they're a real mess. I don't think I'll ever get them clean. [1] What d'you think I should do?

Text G

This is from a transcript of two friends talking about their children. A brief pause is indicated by (.), a number in brackets indicates the length of a pause in seconds, and a vertical line indicates the beginning of simultaneous speech.

> H: yeah well it is the thing is they're um Angie's doing her coursework for her
>   GCSEs and Naomi's doing her coursework for her A levels (.) | yeah   [1]
> M: | yeah
> H: what's Chris doing then did he go is he still working for Jim is he?
> M: yeah he doesn't like it much?

H: oh doesn't he?
M: no no a lot of early starts and late finishes but um no he's not
H: because he was thinking about going to university wasn't he at one point?
M: he was
H: because he could still go couldn't he he doesn't have?
M: he that's what he he says now he's um might do another year
H: oh right
M: and then um reassess because he says he doesn't think he's going to stay there

Source: adapted from a transcript by Stephanie Bishop.

AS English Language

Student answers

Question 1

Study texts A–G. These extracts illustrate different varieties of language use. Discuss the ways in which these texts can be grouped, giving reasons for your choices.

A-grade answer

The texts can be grouped according to register. Texts C, E, F and G are informal while text B has elements of both formality and informality, particularly in the second illustration, in which the scientist's formal register, 'specimen of Felis Catus', is juxtaposed with the informal translation: 'COR — WHAT A NICE MOGGIE!'

On the other hand, text A is a formal letter, informing the recipient that his or her car has been towed away. It uses formal language because it is an official, legal letter and must be unambiguous. It is a standard letter and is formulaic to a degree and must remain impersonal as only the name, date and address would be changed. Text A can be grouped with text D, which also uses formal language. However, although they both have an informative purpose, they have different dual purposes, in that text A is also to instruct and D is to persuade. Text D is a leaflet advertising a personal organiser and it uses formal language as it wishes to create a professional image of the product. The advert could be read by anyone but there is a suggestion that it is aimed more specifically at a businessperson because of the reference to 'missed meetings' and 'memos'.

> 🖉 The candidate makes a good first impression, showing clear understanding of the task and not wasting time with a long introduction. The first grouping is introduced in the opening sentence, which is good exam practice. The candidate understands why text A is formal, and by linking it with text D introduces the idea of grouping by purpose and demonstrates understanding of the term 'dual purpose'. He/she shows a good depth of thought by considering the possibility of a more specific audience.

Text D can also be grouped with text C because they both are IT related and use field-specific lexis. Both texts do this as they are for an audience of computer-literate people, although the lexis of text D is more accessible to the general public than that of C, which is almost jargon only understood by chat room devotees. Text D uses jargon to impress its audience and hopefully to persuade them to buy the organiser, but text C uses it for speed and because there is a shared understanding in this context.

> 🖉 The candidate makes a fluent link between paragraphs. This is done throughout the essay, a technique which suggests evidence of planning. Note the accurate use of the terms 'field specific lexis' and 'jargon'.

Text C can also be grouped with texts F and G because they are all unplanned. Text C is a sequence of messages from a chat room while text G is a transcript of a conversation between two women discussing their children. Text G is obviously unplanned because it uses non-fluent features such as false starts, repetition and fillers. Text G is spoken language, while text C has some features of spoken language but is still a written text, so it could be classed as a cross-boundary text. Text F is spontaneous too but the speaker could have told this story several times, perhaps mimicking a Scottish accent for effect.

> Again, the candidate uses appropriate terminology and is aware of the subtleties of classifying some of these texts. The answer is moving away from the more obvious comments on spoken/written modes. There is also some justified tentativeness in the comments on text F.

Text C can be grouped with text E, as both have non-standard features. Text C has Americanisms, such as 'HOWS YALL DOIN!?' These expressions are quick to use and because the internet and chat rooms are much more established in the USA, the chatters have picked up on them and re-used them. Text E attempts to recreate a Glaswegian accent — *'ye're no* a good man, *ye're just no* a good man' — which could be linked with text F's attempt at dialect.

> The candidate uses 'non-standard' accurately, as it embraces both regional dialect and American borrowings. The dialectal features are highlighted, leaving the examiner in no doubt as to the exact phrases to which the candidate is referring.

A connection between text B and text E is that they both have the purpose of entertaining, although they do have different audiences. Text B's audience is children, whereas text E has an older audience. Text B is trying to convey facts about nature but makes them humorous to create more interest in the topic. It tries to relate to its audience by using critical references to teachers and presenting stereotypical images of scientists and teachers. Text E is an extract from a novel and obviously has an older audience because of its more sophisticated lexis. Even though dialect features are used to create character, the sentence structure is more formal.

> This is a good example of how to convey a large amount of information in one paragraph. The candidate begins with the purpose to entertain, which is the kind of category most students can identify, but manages to cover differences and similarities in audience and register at the same time, showing a commendable economy of language and time.

Texts D, B and A can also be grouped for their use of graphology, but again they use it for different purposes. Text D uses it to persuade the reader to buy the product by showing what the screen will look like, while text B uses graphology to add interest and convey humour. Text A uses a logo to show that it is a reputable company and to give an impression of authority.

AS English Language

🖉 The candidate leaves the most obvious and favourite grouping to the end, and does not simply give a recital of all the different font sizes and illustrations, which most candidates favour, but links graphology to purpose.

🖉 **This is not a perfect answer, but it is certainly worth a grade A. It avoids obvious, simplistic groupings such as spoken and written that most candidates seize upon. The candidate is aware of differences and cross-boundary texts within the chosen groups. The essay is coherent, suggesting evidence of planning. Its approach is systematic, showing understanding and appropriate use of linguistic terminology. The expression is accurate and clear.**

■ ■ ■

C-grade answer

Texts A, B, D and E are all written texts and all four are permanent and planned as well but Text B has some spoken language in speech bubbles. Text C is written in the sense that it is typed onto the computer but it contains many spoken features and if typed quickly is spontaneous and the text will not remain in the chat room for long so it is ephemeral. Text F is spontaneously spoken but has been written afterwards. Text F is ephemeral and text G is too. Text G is spoken and spontaneous.

🖉 The candidate begins with one of the most obvious groupings (spoken and written), but also includes planned and spontaneous. Appropriate linguistic terminology is used, but there is no evidence that the candidate fully understands the terms. For example, the candidate could have identified and discussed the spoken features of text C. The candidate's own expression is rather clumsy, which suggests that the paragraph has been rushed.

Text A is message orientated, as are texts B and D. Texts C, E, F and G are socially orientated. Texts A, E, F and G are all non-technical. Text B is non-technical but there is one technical phrase used: 'Felis catus'. Text C is technical, for example 'chatterz' and 'buffer'. Text D is technical: 'IBM–compatible 486 PC'. Text A is context-free in that the person the text is aimed at should be able to understand everything, but it is context dependent in that the reader will not have explicit understanding and knowledge of 'Section 101 of the Road Traffic Regulation Act 1984'. Text C is context dependent in that the text begins 'yeha that's better hon :))' and without more information we do not know what this is referring to. Text D is context free in that the reader can fully understand what is being advertised, but some of the information is not fully explained, for example 'Mouse 20 MB' would not be understood by people who do not know a lot about computers. Texts B, E, F and G are all context-free and the reader will have explicit understanding of the texts as they are.

> Again the candidate gives possible groupings (message orientated and socially orientated) but without any development, as the answer moves into another grouping (technical and non-technical) immediately. The candidate could have discussed the intended audiences and how this affects the language features of a text, which should form part of a consideration of context. The candidate does, however, provide some effective examples to support the points. The style is unclear and difficult to follow, and some of the terminology is not precise, for example 'technical'.

Texts B, D and E are all non-interactive but text A could be interactive if the letter is replied to as suggested in the text: 'complete and sign the appropriate section on the attached Disclaimer Form and return'. Text C, like text A, is not co-present but it is interactive. Texts F and G are both interactive and face-to-face.

Although the reader is addressed ('you to be the current') in text A, it is not personal because of the reference number and the fact that it begins 'Dear Sir,' without a name and does not end with a name or signature. Text B is personal ('when you don't understand') as is text C ('on ur keyboard') and text D ('to simplify your life'). Texts F and G contain speakers addressing each other in a personal way. Text E addresses the reader with 'Ye wake in', so is personal. On a continuum of formality, texts C, F and G would be towards the informal end whereas texts B and D are of a higher degree of formality. Text A is formal and text E is informal. Texts A, B, D, F and G are standard whereas text C is non-standard ('ehy caps lock') and so is text E ('the words filling yer head').

> In these last two paragraphs the candidate tries to include a great deal of information, but in doing so the essay begins to sound like a list, and becomes dense and difficult to read. Some explanation and development would have helped to clarify the comments. For instance, the term 'direct address' would have shown greater understanding than simply 'addressing each other in a personal way'.

> **This candidate knows about possible groupings and is determined to use as many as possible. The answer might have been a little more successful if it had included fewer groups. It is likely that the candidate went to the examination with a prepared agenda of what to say, and would have done better to have come with a more open mind. This answer would be awarded a grade C.**

Question 2

Take *either* text F *or* text G and any other *two* of the remaining texts. Analyse some of the language features of these texts and explain how these are affected by context. Use some of the following language frameworks where appropriate:
- lexis
- grammar
- phonology
- semantics
- pragmatics
- discourse
- graphology

A-grade answer

Text B is the opening paragraph of a book called *Nasty Nature* from the *Horrible Science* series, written for an audience of older children with the intention of presenting what could be a rather dry, factual subject in a lively and appealing manner. It is informative in purpose and is also entertaining.

The first thing a child will notice is the title. It is written in bold, which draws attention to it. The graphology of the word 'introduction' draws the child in because it is in a child's style of writing. It creates humour and a relaxed style from the outset with its untidy writing style and the animal footprints.

The page opens with three minor sentences — 'Brute force. Beastly behaviour. Animal cunning.' The shortness of the sentences quickens the pace of the text. This grips the child's attention. 'Beastly behaviour' is also clever use of alliteration because it makes it memorable for a child audience. Throughout the page there is repetition of the word 'nasty'. This is a colloquial, informal word choice and possibly a favourite word among children.

Before the picture, there is a row of dots ('...') that creates a pause. This adds drama and excitement to the book while also making what follows more powerful. The clever use of onomatopoeia creates a heightened sense of realism for the reader. Children like being able to sound out the noises such as 'AAAGH' and 'THWACK'.

In the second section of text the author makes an attempt to empathise with the child's point of view: 'We're not talking about your brutish, wolfish, slavering teacher.' This would be quite humorous to a child because many would like to use those adjectives to describe their teachers. The author has tried to get on the child's side, so they feel they are actually having a conversation. This informal style encourages the child to read on. In this sentence the word 'your' is used. This subtle use of direct address backs up the colloquial style.

The use of a rhetorical question also builds up the idea of a conversation. Included in the question is the word 'our'. This is an inclusive word and not only adds to the informal style but shows that the writer and the reader are on the same side.

The picture breaks up the text and makes it easier to read. The characters in the picture are stereotypes of the job or age they portray. For example, the doctor has a white coat, glasses and a bald head.

In the lower drawing, the author cleverly uses bathos (anticlimax) to create humour. The doctor uses field-specific lexis with the term 'Felis catus'. His more sophisticated language builds up to a complicated climax, then the girl says 'Looks more like a cat to me', and we are brought back down to earth by the anticlimax. At the bottom of the extract, the use of 'COR' and 'MOGGIE' is less formal and it is the contrast in the registers of the two speakers that again adds to the humour.

Overall, the piece makes few linguistic demands of a pre-adult reading audience. I would think therefore that the approximate reading age for this extract would be 10–12 years and that it has achieved its purpose of informing and entertaining.

> This is a strong beginning. The essay opens effectively by immediately identifying the dual purpose of the text, and the comments on graphology are linked to the context. The candidate deals with all of the frameworks, including grammar, showing some detailed pragmatic understanding and a sound grasp of terminology. The section on creating humour is particularly impressive, showing real insight into the techniques used by the writer.

Text G is a transcript of two friends talking about their children. They are discussing what their children are doing now they have left school and it is evident throughout that neither person is happy with what they are saying. We can see this because the filler 'um' is used a lot, which shows that they are not assured in what they are saying, and the speech contains several false starts, for example 'did he go is he'. This would indicate that the speakers are backing out of saying something because they realise that they don't want to ask what they were about to say. This is shown by the rephrasing later on of what one speaker was originally going to say: 'he was thinking about going to university'. The speakers could also use the false starts for the simple reason of avoiding bragging about their child. This uncomfortable feel is evident through the many minimal responses such as 'he was' and 'oh right'. This indicates that the speakers don't want to open up and perhaps shows that they care too much or too little about what each child, their own or otherwise, is doing.

Neither speaker is particularly fluent and the conversation appears a little disjointed. For example, 'Yeah well it is the thing is they're um' again shows how uncomfortable the speaker is with the situation and the topic of the conversation. Speaker H has to work very hard to keep the conversation going.

The two friends could possibly be women. This is because men are stereotypically seen as highly unlikely to have a conversation of this sort about their children, whereas women are stereotyped as having this kind of conversation about what their children are doing. According to research, females are also more likely to be concerned to 'save face', which is what seems to be happening here.

> The candidate certainly shows tentativeness in this last paragraph with the comment: 'The two friends could possibly be women'. This demonstrates particularly strong pragmatic awareness. The candidate has evidently read the transcript with some care and is not simply commenting on surface features.

AS English Language

The aim of **text D** is to convince potential buyers that the personal organiser is the one for them. The advertisement is clever because it is aimed at a dual audience. On the left-hand side is the section that appeals to the non-computer literate circle of potential buyers, while the section on the right appeals to computer literate individuals. By addressing both these audiences, sales of the product are likely to be successful.

The first section of the advertisement, which targets non-computer literate people, stands out because it is written in white on black, which draws the reader in. The logo is in the top left corner of the text and since people read from left to right, it is the first thing a reader will notice. The logo consists of the company name, 'Palm', which is circled to add emphasis. The circle has a raised effect, making it appear like a button, which is similar to the product itself. The text style is simple, which suggests how simple life itself would be if you possessed this product.

In the opening sentence, the word 'family' is used, which has homely, caring connotations. It makes the manufacturers sound much less corporate and businesslike. Throughout the whole paragraph the use of direct address is highly effective. Words such as 'you' and 'your' give a sense of the reader being talked to as an individual and create a conversational style. The text then continues to say that this product was designed to simplify 'your life'. The reader then knows the aim of the product. The advert goes on to say: 'No more missed meetings, misplaced numbers or lost notes.' The writer uses minor sentences because they are simple and give connotations of life being simple too. A further list of items — 'agenda', 'memos', 'e-mails' — are keywords in the semantic field of business. They appeal mainly to the business audience but also to other jobs involving IT. Towards the end of the paragraph the advert becomes more personal ('customised to suit your personal needs'), this intimacy with the reader suggesting that his or her needs can be accommodated. To complete the paragraph, the writer personifies the computer as 'the unique companion', making the reader see it in human terms and therefore feeling more inclined to buy one.

The second section of the advertisement, targeted at a computer literate audience, is the size of the actual product, which helps build up an exact image in the reader's mind of the personal organiser he or she could buy. The section is full of field-specific computer lexis. Terms and phrases such as 'IBM-compatible 486PC or higher' and '8MB RAM min' are aimed at a computer literate audience which can understand its meaning and therefore appreciate how good the product is. A bullet point states: '...you'll get all of the organising power of the Palm'. This again emphasises how the product can make your life simpler and better.

In conclusion, the advertisement is very effective in appealing to and associating with a dual audience, using successful techniques to convince diverse potential buyers that this is the personal computer for them.

> This analysis offers comprehensive coverage of the data in text D. The candidate does not waste time at the outset but immediately deals with purpose and then pursues audience, showing insight. Again, the candidate's pragmatic awareness is sound.

> This is a strong A-grade answer. The response to text G is shorter than the other two but the candidate concentrates successfully enough on the pragmatics of the conversation to redeem this imbalance. An analysis of text G which simply pointed out linguistic features without showing this level of understanding would not have merited such a high grade. There is much exemplification, development, clear understanding and accurate use of terminology throughout.

C-grade answer

Text G is informal spoken discourse. At the beginning there are false starts that may suggest that it is unplanned, for example 'yeah well it is the thing is'. There is also a filler which suggests that the person is searching for the correct words: 'they're um Angie's doing her coursework'. There are minimal responses, such as 'yeah', which suggest that two women are speaking, although I cannot be certain.

There are some false starts which show that the speech is spontaneous and the two friends are not sure what to say: 'What's Chris doing then did he go is he still working for Jim is he?' This is also an example of 'hedging' so as to save face.

The conversation becomes disjointed towards the end: 'he that's what he he says how he's um might do another year'. This shows that the person is struggling to find the right words. The repetition in 'he he' again shows that the person is thinking about what to say and 'hedging' so he or she doesn't have to say something negative. It seems that 'M' is uncertain about the facts and is embarrassed at the lack of things 'Chris' is doing compared to 'Angie' and 'Naomi'. The conversation is between people who know each other quite well, so the discourse is informal — 'yeah well it is the thing'.

> The candidate identifies some non-fluency features (false starts and fillers) but needs to develop this by explaining why the speaker is not fluent and why he or she is being so careful over language choices. Correct terminology is used but the reasons for its use are not fully explored. This is only attempted near the end of this section. The candidate seems to be hampered by too much terminology illustrating how terminology must not become an end in itself — it is a tool for exploring ideas. The candidate has sensed the pragmatics of the conversation but seems to have plunged straight into the analysis without first getting an overview of the text.

Text C is informal discourse. It is typed, so it is written discourse, but it has features of speech, for instance 'ehy caps lock'.

In this piece field-specific lexis is used — 'Tittix has quit IRC (Ping timeout).' This can exclude those who don't have much knowledge of computer jargon, suggesting that the people in the chat room are more computer literate than the average person.

There are number and letter homophones used in this text to express the person's views and to save time, for example 'there is a key on ur keyboard' and 'IM FEELING KINDA LOUD 2DAY!'

Within this piece there are Americanisms — 'HOWS YALL DOIN!?' This may be because the internet is used worldwide and often people from different countries mix online and pick up new jargon and non-standard dialect. At the moment Americanisms are seen as prestigious in England.

There are emoticons in this text that express people's feelings, for example 'yeha that's better hon :))' and 'use anticaps :-p'. There are abbreviations which again are timesaving: 'HELLO PPL'.

Some of the people in the chat room appear to be offended by one person's use of capital letters and they single out that person and use sarcasm to quieten them down: 'would u be so kind to press that key so you don't excess us with your CAPS? Thank you.'

> The candidate shows understanding of the genre and makes some good points, for example on the use of Americanisms, using accurate and appropriate terminology. There is more of an attempt to explain its use than there was for text G. However, the candidate's approach could have been more organised — the short paragraphs jump from one point to another, preventing a sense of fluency and sophisticated analysis.

Text B is taken from a book in a series called *Horrible Science,* which is written for older children. The title 'Introduction' has little animal footprints around it which makes it more fun for a child to read. This is good use of graphology. It starts off with a list of three very short and quick sentences. These are a good way of keeping children interested, as long sentences may bore them.

Another clever way the text keeps a child's attention is by not including too much writing and using comical pictures to show exactly what is meant. This is a good way of educating children without them realising. The use of onomatopoeia, such as 'thwack', keeps the child's attention, because children often enjoy stories with visual images and sound effects they can repeat in their head.

Attention is also kept by referring to teachers as 'brutish', 'wolfish' and 'slavering'. This is a good way of interesting children because they find it humorous when teachers are compared to comical things. The text uses speech bubbles which add to the fun and comical effect by including humorous translations.

> The candidate has wasted time at the beginning of this section by merely copying the rubric. This is never advisable unless you are going to expand on it. The answer does, however, demonstrate a keen awareness of how language features are matched to the target audience. The candidate makes a brief reference to the educative purpose of the text, but this could have been explored further. The final paragraph makes two good points but neither are developed fully. There is not enough discussion of language in this answer.

> **Overall, this response shows enough understanding of the texts to achieve a grade C, but lacks the systematic, organised approach which is the mark of an A-grade candidate.**

Groupings exercise response

The Content Guidance section of this guide contains a set of data to use as practice for arranging texts into appropriate groups, in order to help you prepare for question 1 of the Introduction to the Study of Language exam (see pp. 28–33). Below is an A-grade response to the data. It was written in 35 minutes after an initial period of reading and note making. It is not a perfect answer, but it does show how the texts can be grouped and how a cohesive essay can be produced. You may have come up with some similar groupings or you may have found groupings different from the candidate here.

A-grade answer

Classed by mode, there are three texts that could be speech — D, F and H — but these are also cross-mode as they have all been written down. Text H is a written script to be spoken on stage and was therefore planned thoughtfully. Text F is part of a spontaneous conversation that would have been ephemeral if it had not been written down. Although text D is spoken, the interviewer has a set formula for the questions, so the discussion is to some extent planned and could be grouped with the written texts.

> The candidate identifies a grouping but shows due tentativeness in the choice of language — for example, 'that could be speech'. The response avoids dogmatism and instead explores possibilities.

Texts A, B, C, D and G all have an informative purpose, although text A, and to some extent text G, are instructive too. Texts B, E and G are also dual-purpose texts, because they are trying to sell membership and goods as well as giving information to the reader. Text B uses the dinosaur drawings as part of this persuasion while text E uses the image of the chair. These images are cleverly linked to the lexical choice; for instance, the words 'T-rex' and 're-hatch' in text B are connected to the dinosaur drawings. There is therefore an entertainment element in these two texts, although only text H was written for that purpose.

> Note the phrase 'to some extent' — again, the candidate is avoiding dogmatic statements. The acknowledgment of dual-purpose elements shows that some careful thought has taken place.

Graphology plays an important part in some of the texts. Text G has an accompanying picture of the product (not shown). The font sizes are varied and suited to their purpose in texts E and G, and the overall layout of text C underlines its warning. The graphology of text A is typical of a recipe. (The crafty advertising for Asda within this graphology is also notable — this is another purpose for text A.) Similarly, text H's layout is typical of its literary genre. All these written texts are different, but they are all making the graphology work for the writer's intended purpose.

> This response does much more than simply itemise all the graphological features. The candidate sees that graphology is important in some texts but has to be different to suit the purpose. The sentence about Asda's 'crafty advertising' should really have been in the purpose section, but the candidate has managed to work it in here.

As far as register is concerned, there is a broad spectrum within these texts. Text C is very formal, using standard English, field-specific lexis and formal syntax. Texts F and B are the least formal. Text B uses some of the features of direct speech found in text F, such as contractions like 'we've' (text B) and 'you'll' (text F) and the hint of an accent in text F, with 'av' and 'mi'. Text G also employs clichéd phrases such as 'for peace of mind', 'do your best', 'it's wise' to create an informal register and a relationship with the reader. Interestingly, text H contains many informal speech features but its genre is formal.

> It is always difficult to write about register because links are not always precise. The candidate overcomes this by acknowledging that there is a range before trying to identify informal language features to link the texts together.

Texts H and C are permanent texts, whereas all the others are ephemeral. Texts D and F are only permanent because they have been transcribed. All the other texts are easily discarded. The flyer (text B) could easily be thrown away unread, as could the envelope (text G). Perhaps some readers might keep the recipe (text A) or the programme (text E). These people would probably belong to a specific audience group interested in cooking or music. Text H would probably appeal to an audience of theatre-goers or literature students. Apart from texts D and F, whose audiences are only the actual participants, the texts in this selection have very specific audiences. Even the flyer for the leisure club is directed towards ex-members within a certain area, and the audiences for texts B and G are the companies' existing customers.

> Many candidates write too vaguely about audience. By specifying the audiences for each text, the candidate is showing a high level of understanding.

> **This answer covers a wide range of groups and there is depth of comment and development. The candidate uses appropriate examples from the data and writes coherently. Not every possible grouping is covered, but taking exam conditions into account, this essay would be awarded a grade A.**